Tunnels of the Mind

a collection of poems

Peter Tomlinson

Published by bluechrome publishing 2004

2 4 6 8 10 9 7 5 3 1

First published in Great Britain in 2004 by
bluechrome publishing
An Imprint of KMS Ltd
PO Box 109;
Portishead, Bristol. BS20 7ZJ

www.bluechrome.co.uk

A CIP catalogue record for this book is available from the British
Library

ISBN   1-904781-81-0

Dedication

To my wife Margaret, the sweetness of my mind.

Also to the editors of 80 or so magazines in UK and abroad who have used my work and to the adjudicators who sometimes let me win their competitions.

Contents

Tunnels of the Mind

The City

The decision to leave was not sharply made:
it developed slowly and was suddenly there.
The city seemed heartless and cold that night;
the only warmth it offered was in its darkness.

Houses paraded in straight featureless lines
with front doors concealing private tyrannies.
His way was marked by clinicised trees
confined by stone and cruelly planted in concrete soils.

He walked aimlessly on streets of voices, music,
laughter and hidden pockets of despair.
The city was in pause, holding its wounded day.
Distant sounds whispered like bad thoughts in empty
minds.

Rain distorts the reflections of a city cloaked in cold
darkness.
People dehumanise and hide behind sameness
in their living cemetery.
He will leave the city now, and never return.

The Remains of an Old Lane

Along this winding sunken lane,
going from nowhere to nowhere else,
there is an endless tale to tell
of generations as they rose and fell.

Of all who passed this way before,
one still lies beneath this heavy stone.
The Saxon lord of hereabouts;
of eternal fame he had no doubts.

A Norman baron came this way,
campaigning in a foreign land,
with a captive people to subdue
and tax them for Duke William's due.

Struggling home with a sword thrust deep,
a soldier died by this ancient oak.
He saw a king who lost and ran,
and raised a cheer, that Cromwell man.

Along this winding sunken lane,
trudged those in bondage to the mill.
A cruel earthly colony of hell
that scarred and darkened valley and fell.

Lads of the Great War went this way
to battle it out in khakied ranks.
And after them were brothers to come;
but most were lost in mud on the Somme.

The lane sank deeper from countless feet
as history marched its relentless way.
Some to hunt and others to poach,
till the city began to encroach.

And soon this lane will be no more,
just a line on an ancient map.
From progress there is no escape;
a new silence now beneath a cityscape.

Semolina Days

a forties childhood.

Echoes from hazy years
of a non ending time;
dismal school of brown tiles,
halls smelling of dinners,
hard seats
and the fear of being wrong.
Indignities of childhood stoically endured.

A world of cold corridors with loud closing doors,
classes chanting tables,
or singing dreary hymns
to an old piano.
Helpless cries lost in
concrete playground yells,
grazed knees, tears and childhood smells.

Glimpsing a world of drab places,
shabby life and dads in demob suits.
A time of immediate impulse:
throwing stones,
scraping out the treacle tin,
hitting girls,
spending milk money on broken biscuits.

Sunday School Treat with an apple and an orange each.
Cap and jerkin,
Fair Isle pullover,
sagging socks,
rummaging on bombsites.

Saturday afternoon flicks
and sing every Sunday for One and Six.

Links with an earlier self recede
as images fragment behind the mind.
The child's world spins away
as the distance between us lengthens
and small windows of recollection close.

The child and his time are cast beyond my reach.

Trailing Shadow

Casting your mind back
to places of childhood
is never to have left,
only a slightly changed picture
in a new frame.

The retrospective gaze
meets the forward view,
at the limits of an old posterity.

Two strangers meet at the fulcrum
where the future became the past.
Invisible tethers, pulled to severance,
trail behind like strings in the wind,
beckoning to reclaim the last seed
that fell from a dying tree
to germinate in the decaying remains.

The former identity falls away.
It fades as a distorting shadow
and becomes unrecognised,
as the mould fashioned by the child
is broken.

Turn away to what future is left
and tread the trackless years
to wherever …

Boy Soldier under Air Attack

Crawl into the ground
and cower in bone-scraping fear.

Taste dirt in your mucus
as you press your face into the mothering earth
in dehumanising terror
and curse the uniform
that stole your innocence.

Thin streaks of aerodynamic menace,
the product of human genius,
roar overhead
like screams echoing
in the dungeons of hell.

Your vitality and youth sacrificed:
a puny irrelevance
in global policy.

Cry 'it's me! … it's ME! …'
But none will hear

and none will know.

Leftover World for Sale

A used planet is offered
with vacant possession
to any new species
that may evolve.

Much sought after position in the solar system
blessed with all the requirements of life.

But buyers beware,
ocean and wilderness need attention.
Structural fundamentals have been tampered with
and the elements of life altered.
Previous occupants given to the sin of arrogance.

New owners sought without avarice,
or a greedy propensity to change things.
The world can wait until new creatures evolve
as Man's span was merely a blink of a celestial eye.

House Clearance

There wasn't much to show for a life,
a few bits and bobs
and a medal or two.

He'd been old for years
and quietly died of tiredness.

There was no one close;
he was a charge on the council
and dealt with on a rota.

There was a stain on the carpet
where meals-on-wheels found him
and brought the police round.

Forgotten relatives came to take their pick:
the gold watch he got from the works when he finished
and a fancy tray he'd brought back from Rhyl.

A dozen bin liners cleared him out
and what was left went in the skip.

The new people arrived with their lives to lead
and decorated him out of the picture.

Only the creaky door he couldn't fix
remained to tell of his passing.

City Churchyard

Villages became suburbs
as the town gorged on itself
spreading its entrails ever outwards.

The dark stoned church whose gothic spire
had pointed defiantly at flying bombs
was abandoned by a downsizing faith
and became a warehouse.
Only the gravestones survive:
ornamental remains of a lost reverence.

Developers will clear away these sacred selves,
with silent screams unheard beneath a prime site,
denying post-mortal rights.
Fading names peer through silent eyes
above the weeds
and whisper to be remembered.

Indifference negates the lives
of once vital people;
we can never retrace our steps
if we lose our way.

The hurrying world will bundle them up
into skips or municipal pits
and they will be as if they never were.
Sterile records will take the place of memory.

And the remaindered people
will slide towards their own anonymity
without ritual or ceremony.

An Ancient Site

Like a tortured scream in the night,
unseen their passion soared and was lost.
Darkness closed the vacuum of life,
and a generation had passed.
Footsteps in rock lost definition,
and monuments declined,
washed and harassed by unending years,
and the dust that made the men came to rest
in the cavity of his image.

And the sun rose again.

Brothers' Parting

*Written at The Brothers' Parting Stone in the English Lake District,
where William and John Wordsworth parted for the last time*

Grisedale Tarn feels heavy
under the cloak of melancholy,
condemned to early darkness
by surrounding hills
and short stormy days.

A rising wind tugs against the grass
in grievous remonstrance.
Small rocks protrude from the ground
like drowning men gasping for air.
Sheep worry a sparse living
from leathery undergrowth
eking their way through the short,
unforgiving life allowed them.

A stream torrents its way
from Grisedale Tarn
down towards Patterdale.

I watch the ghostly drama
from a shadowy past,
as Brother John, a man of sword and sea,
picks his way down the tortuous path,
with a sad backward glance,
to meet his end off Portland.

William retraces his steps from that gaunt stone
around Grisedale Tarn
deep in thoughts of the Prelude
to distract a parting sadness
no comfort can redress.
The brothers tread their separate ways
along paths their fates decreed.
Only the birds watched their last embrace
in this wild empty place.

William follows the homeward stream
chattering its way down the mountain
towards the welcoming lights of Grasmere
and the warmth of Dove Cottage fireside.

The Poet long remembered that last sad adieu
of brothers who went their separate ways,
to meet again only in dreams of boyhood days.

Tunnels of the Mind

It was only the next day
or so it seemed.

They were all pleased,
as if I'd been away a long time
and they were glad for me now.
I couldn't break through to them,
I had no movement.
They were beyond distance.

My bed was being made.
They had a routine,
always two of them.
I was moved without words.
They never looked at my eyes
to see right in.
Others looked on.

There is no pain in the tunnels.
My mind is fragmented
and dispersed in times and places.

We crossed once
when they were making the bed
but I don't know where that was.

His people stopped coming.
He became a wanderer in the tunnels,
lost in anti-time.

Three years later,
a clinical decision was made.

Tiger Spent

When did the world leave you behind
and carry on without you?
Everything moves so fast for you now
and machines are where people used to be.

Remember when you felt the wind in your hair,
storming out of El Alamein,
your body armoured with confidence
and indestructible youth,
moving with thoughtless fluency?

Remember when you tigered ashore in Normandy?
Those first thousand yards were like a million miles.
You lost Nobby and Bob there,
and Staff Sergeant Wills!

But today's people don't know of your time
or what it was like for you.
In the slow years now,
a time of diminishing affinity:
a bypassed irrelevance.

Notes on Beauty

Beauty needs no eye to see it,
no voice to praise or tell of it
or hand to touch it.

Beauty links together
all who have eyes to see
and minds free from the fetters of futile enterprise.

It will be there for us
when we cast aside
the shackles of everyday life.
It waits to cool the brow
and soothe the aching mind.

Beauty does not compete
or demand attention.
It is there waiting,
always waiting,
for us to find.

Beauty is the soul in tears of joy.

A Post-War Childhood

I often wander in the haze
of childhood memories:
a place of bombed buildings
and the blitzed remains of my town.
Running wild in the ruins of wrecked homes,
burrowing into damp cellars
and collecting stained glass
from the skeletoned church.
Roaming the wasteland
in make-do clothes
and a pocket full of stones
for rival gangs.
Dodging the scuffers
and running home to hide.
School dinners sparse and tasteless,
no choice: eat what you're given
or go without.
Climbing over the dock wall
for sherbet and monkey nuts
from the Yankee boats.

The winter of '47 -
a time of punishing cold.
Waiting at the gas works
for a sack of coke
to take home on a pram.
Rumours that a shop has bananas
spread amongst the queuing mothers.
Bananas, one per family,
next week, always next week!

Queue, queue for everything.
Signs in shop windows:
No Meat Today.

The ache of anticipation
spun out a childhood
of sweet-tasting promises
that would always be tomorrow.

The Seasons

It is a sad time in the stillness of autumn;
the land is at rest after summer's vigour
and trees shed their fading finery
to clothe the forest floor.
A hint of cold sharpens the edge of the hurrying wind
and southerning instincts stir urgent wings overhead.
Nature's palette reflects a melancholy season
with the sombre tints of graceful decay
in failing light.

Winter's face looks narrow-eyed
through the piercing wind
and sighs in resignation at the barren land.
Winter will leave stark the skeleton tree
which creaks in bondage to thoughtless cold.
Lifeless run the furrows
walked by those to the struggle born
who dream of warm summers
and barns of smiling plenty.
A time of longing behind cottage lights.

Spring has a child's Christmas morning face
which smiles in the winds
that rush to summon all life from sleep.
It brings the news of approaching summer
and sets tall trees waving to distant hills,
as early leaves applaud the promise of life.
The dormant seed is roused in the mothering earth.
It uncoils with untried strength
and stretches eagerly towards the sun.

Summer has the broad smile of promise fulfilled.
The trees whisper behind the wind
in the land of the big sky.
A sea of languid grass turns its silvered edge to the sun
and scatters in the playful wind.
Clouds like a child's vapoured breath
hang in gentle winds
that caress warm land with their cooling shadows
while crowded hedgerows watch the dance in Monet fields.

House with Vacant Possession

A home no more,
deserted and not wanted,
standing in its own neglected graveyard
looking sad and vacant through nude windows.

A once vibrant dwelling
emptied of its soul
sinking into sad silence
with the voice of passed people
fading into the damp of neglect.

Noises sneak through bare rooms
as the house creaks and settles,
easing itself into a new abandoned posture.

A searching wind rattles the windows at night
seeking out newly emptied spaces
where memories linger,
and people-sounds fade like half remembered tunes.

Cross Your Own Shadow

It was in my after-time
that I went from here
and returned to the time of my youth.
They were all there,
expecting me.

Smells of childhood things
and a young mother tending me.
Sights and sounds once known
were lost
but were known again.
The hollow fears were there
and the mouth that couldn't speak.

I saw people from my wakening.
I knew them, behind their masks.
Their faces moved
but I didn't know if they were crying or not.

From there I trod the familiar path
through ungathered moss
where our ways crossed.
Memories fade behind,
like footsteps in melting snow.

I am both the child of myself
and the man in the crowd.
I met myself many times on the way.

Black and White War

Recalling the films of Humphrey Jennings

It is a black and white time
that flickers on the screen.
A war of distant memory,
of lornful music,
and clouds shadowing across the landscape.

Determined cliffs,
white and straight,
reach upwards
beyond the grasping hands of the sea.

It is a drab world,
its youth harnessed to the nations will.
But a time of warm friendships and shared cigarettes.
Sweet tea in tin mugs,
and people whistling while they work.

Faces stiff in stoical defiance,
tired, their decency interrupted
by feigned barbarism.
People of private emotions sing together
as they forge weapons to arm themselves.
Pulsating factories pour smoke
that lingers over towns and valleys.
Gothic fingers rise from rubbled towns
and point brokenly to the sky.

Cold lightless dusk,
haunted by the siren's ghostly call.
Nights pass in comfortless companionship,
with shared melodies and unhurried voices,
communing around the wireless
hearing words of determination
from a stuttering king.

The film recedes from dark streets,
and sounds are lost in the quiet watch of the night.
The laboured day draws to another close
in the sunset's promise of dawn.

A lone Lancaster,
silhouetted by moonlight,
drones away into the night
and the watchful Spitfire
lurks behind darkening clouds.

A fighting nation
rests its determined brow
and we reflect:
was all the anguish worth
what we are now?

Balkan Cycle

A heavy silence hangs over the land;
a dirty shroud of guilt has descended.
It penetrates hidden corners of the mind
as a mist threads through a forest,
and worries at the thoughts of men.
In this land they avoid newly turned earth:
the evidence is shallow laid
beneath Balkan soil
that Man did not advance beyond the savage.

Some quietly slipped away
to live the lie of innocence,
remembering dark moments
behind the mask of anonymity
and crimes that defy telling.

The young choke on their tears
and women wail with aching breasts,
overwhelmed by the demonic strength of hate.
The old sit behind vacant eyes
that have seen too much
and have no focus on hope.

The cycle cannot be broken
while memory lives.
Again in the fertile minds of children
the seeds of hate are sown.
The bitter earth is soured
by unforgiving elders
obsessed with vendetta

and perverted history,
whilst priests chant their godsongs.

But the people of the dead are the masters now
and the next generation prepares for war.

The Cavern Club, Liverpool

The beat and strum of new music
echoed through the dark canyons of drab Liverpool
amid the murky lights
of the old Merseysippi.
Deep in the cellars of the Cavern Club
pulsed the heartbeat of emerging youth.

It broke the shackles of a disciplined time
when adults ruled the moment
with harshly disciplined schools
and military conscription.

Rhythm soared through the bodies
of the speak-back generation,
reaching always a little further
to unfettered exuberance,
and a frenzied run onto the plateau of life.

Gone now,
vanquished to the vacuum of memory
leaving future generations dancing in its shadow.

Lost Intent

Unreal people playing at being real
in a world of middling men
with only the skills of the seething city:
a herd held in mesmeric helplessness
by the promise of immediate things.

It was always his intent
to escape from agony's acre,
where people squat in the ruins of their lives,
to cut the fetters of convention,
to chase the wind
and run down into the valley of life.

But he dwelt too long
in the remote corners of his imagination,
wandering as a lost child
in the corridors of deception.

His intent unresolved and lost,
he joined the sad and the solitary
shuffling through the age of self-delusion.

War Memorial

Do not presume a willing sacrifice,
a glorious end of youth in death.
Don't patronise us in this way
and tell us it was nobly done.

We advanced in close regimental order
heads down and faces masked with fear.
Not heroes, just bewildered young men.

Life was torn from our flesh
by the jagged steel of random shot.
We sank to the ground and screamed
hate
that you put us to this.

Uniqueness bled dark red from us
to mingle dirtied and prematurely spent,
lost for ever in Death's obscenity.

Rites of Passage

It was a time of immediate thoughts
and desires akin to childhood,
when the trivial was important
and the important trivial.

But that was Christmases ago.

A tuber, grotesque and ungainly
in the earth,
emerges to the surface
to take final form
with uncertain prospect.

But it was so confusing.

Worrying at the reins,
you escaped the byred life.
No longer fashioned by parents
in the adjunctive years,
you took the measure of the world.

But it seemed an age.

From whirlpool to rapids
you struck out with puny strokes.
The main world pulled you apart
and reassembled you to its preferred specification,
sending you scurrying back sometimes
with hurts and dormant fears
to the warmth of infancy.

But you soon lost your way.

Sea and Sky

Corpulent clouds robed in purest white
sail the blue ocean,
the stately argosies of the sky
wafting where they will
to fall demurely below horizons.

Whispering tides caress the beach
where the land crowds to the shore
with cliffs and caves
of ancient cataclysm.
Subterranean rumbles warn of power at rest.

The sea changes its face,
following the moods of the sky
in perfect mirror.

The winds blow stronger
and begin to worry the trees.
Men look to the sky with wizened eye
and small boats run to harbour.
Clouds change their clothes
for stormy garb
and race across the wide ocean
cloaking the world in darkness.

Night stalks the storm-darkened world
and men shiver as they turn away.
Shore lights flicker in cold reflection
as the sea and sky are joined in seamless distance.
The sea inks into the night
keeping its secrets.

Heritage Lost

I have often wandered in the hills of Wales
listening for the voice of my ancestors.
It is a tear soaked-land of melancholy memories
and people singing mournfully to themselves.
I have felt the anguished rocks beneath my feet
and set my eyes to the horizons
that my people must once have seen.
But their song and poetry is lost to me
and I remain deaf to their whispers.

And so I will wander the hills of Wales and gaze
into deep valleys at ruined cottages and lonely settlements.
I will see the menacing slag heaps that towered over them,
and the pit heads that swallowed their lives,
coughing them up each night
broken in poverty and servitude.
The toil of my fathers hewed this land to sadness
but what, I ask myself, is there of them in me?

I hear the strange language of my fathers.
Their music caresses my thoughts like an unremembered
dream.
But where in my mind must this old language lie?
How deeply buried are the shared memories
of lore and legends that I cannot bring to mind?
Like a hunger that cannot be fulfilled I am left in emptiness.
I am cast in the mothering earth of Wales,
but where in the song can I find myself?

Pictures in a Newspaper

I am not a cruel man but I must
turn away from this starving child.
    Large eyes
    protruding belly,
    rags.

I am not an indifferent man but I must
ignore the blind man's vacant stare.
    White eyes,
    imploring hand,
    sores.

I am not a callous man but the tethered bear
must mean nothing to me.
    Chain through mouth,
    pained face,
    blood.

That sick woman on page four wanting:
    the change in my pocket,
    my next cup of coffee,
    the price of a packet of crisps.

That's all she asks and another billion like her.
But what more can I do?
I have a standing order every month for:
    exhausted donkeys,
    clean water supply,
    medical aid,
    pandas and whales.

What more can I do?
Sell up and go and work with lepers?
What if we all did that? There's too many of them.
I must remain prosperous so I can help. I think that's right.
Hope so.
Our overseas aid, something-point-something of GDP?

Always the pictures escalate, always chasing
the contrived indifference of my defence.
But look at that sweat shop child in rags, making my shoes
Perhaps I won't buy them.
But then he will starve!

I must turn away to protect myself,
but I can feel their eyes between my shoulder blades.

An English Country Churchyard

The old church lies heavily in gentle folds of earth.
Clad in the moss of centuries,
it mocks our fleeting time.
Stark is the gate of final departure
where pall-bearers take their rest
and vicars begin their mournful song.

Stone monuments that mark lost ages
sink slowly into the beckoning earth.
The sexton's wound finally heals,
and the endless hazard of time
slowly erases the names of those remembered
only by those who are themselves forgotten.

Poorly marked is the grave of the man to the struggle born,
who paid his debt to toil
and bequeathed subservience to his sons.
A life's labour on the cruel cycle of the year
until broken in want, and the land was poorer by a man.

A cross with poppies records the lost sons of the parish,
of families dismembered by foreign wars to lie in alien soils.
Summoned by their betters who officered their ranks
and spent them as required,
the small change of conflict.

Marked also, the graves of servants
whose lives were stolen by servitude,
returned to dust on the light step of innocence
or the heavy drag of guilt.
They lived and died in sure and certain dread:
a passive acceptance of what they were told.

Tributes fade and wither to dust
and the churchyard sinks into a neglected sleep.
The anguished earth corrupts lost passions that stir no
more.
Futile hope and memory cut in stone
crumble and die,
abandoned in a land of lost belief.

Stately Home

A Poem for Two Voices

Hope you can all hear me. The house was built
by the second baronet and the obelisk was brought
back from his grand tour and he had this ceiling
painted and that's him there by Gainsborough it's
beautiful. Please move on and try to stay together.

The aristocrats' loot spaced out in sumptuous rooms.
It was carried back from Rome and Florence in crates
of backbreaking shape to tickle the master's fancy
and promote smart conversation in the drawing room.

And here they dined off twelve courses once when
the king came and then into the private theatre for
plays and charades and that's her ladyship there by
Van Burgh and the young heir who fell at Waterloo.
Look at the French clock as you pass through the room.

Deferential tourists shuffle through magnificent rooms
like sinners looking upon the wonders of heaven.
They know nothing of Molly aged twelve who crawled into cupboards
to cry away her youth and escape the housekeeper's strap.

And her present ladyship often comes into the tea-room
and speaks to the visitors just like you or I would
and that's a photograph of them at the coronation in
their robes and coronets standing in a group at the Abbey.
That's another French clock. Please move on and stay
together.
Ignore the five-pound tour and feel for the arthritic

servants who carried dishes up these winding stairs.
Skilled in the preparation of food and the anticipation
of wishes and whims, they owned not a moment of their day.

The third baronet became the first earl who married an
American heiress from Detroit and played cards with the
Prince of Wales at Windsor but had to go abroad after a
duel and that's the coat he wore and you can see the hole.
Admire the porcelain dishes in the cabinet as you pass by.

They were the silent ones, the unnoticed ones who left
their mark only in a walnut shine or a scoured sink,
their aching toil cast to uncertain memory;
their lives stolen by service. I whisper to their shadows.

Auschwitz

There was a man,
the spawn of evil circumstance,
who made the world his victim.
His portents went unread
by the wisdom of the day.

He left a stain on the minds of men,
that can never be erased:
a thought that broke the bounds of reason.

Today the quiet hangs around this place
like a dirty shroud thrown over a corpse.
The silence funnels the mind
through the ever present past.

The destroyers of hope
prowled this place
where compassion died.
Horror became routine policy
in the normalisation of evil.

We have all been to Auschwitz
in our undefended dreams,
to wander numbed
and tight of mind
like the shuffling ones before us
for whom it was real.
Tormented beyond hope,
they were abandoned
by whatever gods
they thought they had.

And down the ages will slink tainted man,
hiding from the thought
that what he once was,
he has become again.

Leftover Town

remembering Dylan Thomas

Dawn creeps across grey slated roofs
spilling into another put-the-kettle-on morning.
Doors open to admit cats
and let out dogs to urinate on iron lamp posts.
The sun rises and surveys the leftovers
of this little Welsh town,
cut off and dying since they closed the pit.
The people of Same Street
ease themselves into the corset of their routine.

Gladys stands before the mirror
in her cheap satin catalogue nightdress.
She looks at the photograph of Dai
who went to the Gulf War.
Some say he was killed
but others know better.

Bed and Breakfast Minnie
at Sea View with her fake china tea service
and butter dish brought back from Rhyl.
She dusts the Vacancies sign in her window
and props it up with the curtain.

Bert the Blackboard in his chalk stained jacket
eats his cornflakes noisily
and leaves for another drab classroom day.

Hughie the Hymn longs for Sunday
when some come for Jesus
others for the singing
and a few to hear him preach.

Mrs Jones makes her way to clean the church
passing the grave of her Tom,
the baritone and miner,
who sang his last note at the Valleys Festival
before the dust choked the music out of him.

The day draws on in dreary sameness
and replicated weeks.
At night the men sing mournfully into their beer,
eyes glazed remembering the vibrant times.
'Nothing ever happens around here, you know.'
The town died when the Royal Artillery left in 1945
and the pit closed in Thatcher's time.

The deep resonance of their voices
drifts out across the dusky roofs
beyond the slag heap that hovers over them
and out over the hills
where their ancestors lived before the coal.

Their song mingles with the mists in the high crags
where hawks hover and glide down the wind.
The new motorway creases through the valley
shunting the little town into the back ways of life.

The evening shadows cloak the town returning to its
dreams.

Judas

I know my name will be spat down the centuries
from faces uglied with disgust and hate.

But it had to be now.
It had to be tonight.

The silver burns into my hands
dirtied with the filth of apparent betrayal.

My friends' eyes narrow as they look at me;
contempt surrounds me like the foul breath of demons.

But it had to be now.
It had to be tonight.

It is the hour that history waits to start
and write the future in His name.

We could not have returned to Galilee
and preached to fishermen and cured the sick.

It had to be now.
It had to be tonight.

He knew this was his hour sent
when our fates would cross and kill us both.

I slink away and hide in this my greatest sacrifice,
no comfort for me in my name.

It had to be now.
It had to be tonight.

They dragged him away and only I knew
what his face said to me.

I saw there were thanks in those eyes,
because he knew.

It had to be now.
It had to be tonight.

Parallel Life

I am filled with a curious melancholy
as if my parallel self
is undergoing some great sadness.

Maybe he is in abandonment
and all around him is hollowness,
his probing hands finding nothing.

Does he search for me
as I search for him?

How close can we be
on our different sides of time?
Never to confront,
always within feeling,
but never to touch.

What unknown dimension do we share,
each a shadow to the other
in our oblique worlds?

Maybe I feel his joy
and share his fears,
and fill him sometimes
with a curious melancholy.

Finished Symphony

Silently the dust planet lingers
naked of atmosphere
and prey to cosmic wind.
Meteorites disturb its cindered skin
and the faint footprints of forgotten Man
are filled with the debris of a decaying earth.

The cold of endless space
stills the last languid tears
that oozed dirty red
from the cooling centre
and the surface crumbles away
into the crushing void.

But perchance, in a breath of familiar warmth
the human essence
will return just once more
from beyond the edge of anti-time
where thought has yet to travel.
and cast its all feeling eye
over the world that spawned Man
in physical crudity
before the end that was foretold.

Earth will then fall away,
its purpose fulfilled.

Answer Phone

Her semi-focussed eyes
gazed at one spot on the wall.
It generated no thought,
but it seemed to come closer.
Her body was slowed by cold,
as terminal inertia,
unseen and unfelt,
permeated her frailty.

The phone ringing in some distant place
disturbed her immediate self,
but did not stir her sluggish mind.

Hello mum ... having a little shut eye?
... things a bit hectic today ... you know how it is!

Time hung around her
between shallow sleeps.
Child smells,
as wetness dried to stiff discomfort.

People dead to memory
played just below her mind
but had no shape or sound.
Children became adults:
confusingly different people

Yes, all right Stephen, I'm, coming! .... Kids!
Give me a ring if you want anything.

He would always ring if he could,
from outside the barracks.
Just saying little things.
How recent a long time ago seems
when there is so little between.
She couldn't cry hard enough
to bring him back.

Well, mum, bye now.
I'll try and get over to see you the weekend ....

This room was her final world
and then there was only the chair.

She lived outside her body now,
in a world of confused memories,
until she left herself
with a soundless name
on her quivering lip.
Her last tear dried on her cheek
in her final stillness.

Piano Bar

Keys stained by nicotined fingers
tobaccoed breath and smoke,
desultory notes drifting
into beery indifference
across the piano bar,
hardly penetrating
the wall of trivial conversation
and perfunctory applause.

The pianist in crumpled suit
smiles at the off-key drunk in the corner
tormenting the memory of an old song.

The evening drones on
and the pianist loses himself in dreams
of Viennese concert halls
and the magnum opus that never was.

Legitimate Military Target

The foreign face of a conscripted boy
from little-heard-of-land
stares out from a western newspaper.
He is clothed in a uniform of drab denim
hanging loosely on bony shoulders.

Poorly fed and cast randomly to his fate,
a bewildered youth,
trapped by the amorality of the squad.

Weapons, heavy in his puny arms,
dangle grotesquely from his body.
A legitimate military target,
stripped of innocence by a uniform.
A dictator's pawn,
expendable and replaceable
from his teeming people.

No conscience to spare for him.

Overseas Draft 1916: Dover Station

The old station at Dover is now a car park and departure lounge for cruise ships.

Shunted into the ante-room of hell,
an impersonal, shell-like building
of iron girders and brick,
trains endlessly disgorge tired youth,
bewildered boys
dressed in ill fitting khaki
and burdened with kit bags.

The troops form lines to shouts of rank,
and curt commands,
'Come on lads, get fell in'.

Locomotives clank and strain
cursing the condemned with hissing steam
and return for another batch,
another intake:
the sons of unfranchised mothers.

Stamping boots,
click and rattle of equipment,
comforted only by the nearness of each other.
Whispered promises to stay together,
'They won't split us up, will they?'

Last hurried letters home,
'I'm all right, mum.'

Silent thoughts,
unspoken fears
eased by the irreverent camaraderie of youth.

The green shoots
of an early English spring
paraded for slaughter
in the dreaded unspoken assumption
that life now begins to end.

They marched in step
to the death of innocence
on the Somme.

Reunion

The old boss was there:
wanting to be one of us now.
It was strained
but we passed him round.
His wife felt out of it:
sitting with her sherry, smiling on cue.
They left early.

I was talking to a guy
who thought I was someone else,
wasn't sure about him either.
but we all like to be remembered.

Raucous laughter punched the air
dying away quickly
in 'remember the time' conversations:
a strained willingness for togetherness.
Small groups feeling their way
along tenuous threads of memory.

Few stayed until the end,
the younger ones mostly.

Must do it again next year,
yes… we must… sure…

Talking Hands

Warmth-seeking hands
rummaging inside her woolly cardigan,
fingers out of true
with arthritic disfigurement,
skin taut across purpled veins.

Hands that miracled the wartime ration
to spread across hungry mouths,
smacked the child to life
and wiped the eye
of the endless tear.

Broken parchment skin
on hands that scrubbed and skimped
eked and coped
and comforted her dying man.

Worn out, faded and gone
her image pressed in the bible of our memory.

Journey with My Grandfather

Take me with you through your time
and show me the horrors you knew.
You say there are things I must see.
You are the father of my mind
and I still feel your hand on my shoulder,
still see your face from a child's upward look.

There are skeleton trees
and smoke, and stones thrown high in chaotic waves.
We stand on the rubble heap of a village
and see the whole battle area.
The land is sick and barren;
it groans with unremitting pain.
Armies spread across the landscape
with their machines
and contrivances of steel and barb
busying themselves in death and pain.
The land is infested with termite men
burrowing like maggots in the carcass of a dying world.

The sound of their vile play is everywhere.
It carries to the furthest feeling
and echoes in the vacuum of snuffed-out life.
You turn my eyes to see wounded men cowering in shell
holes.
They are insects, dirtied and writhing,
in a hole trodden by men's non-thinking.
You make me look at them,
children of a brain-damaged world, crying inadequate tears.
Can we leave now, grandfather?
Can we quit this place?

We leave the wasteland together
and walk silently over pits of broken youth.
Tread softly, you say,
and do not press dirt into clear eyes
which still peer at the sky.
Do not disturb the earth,
for they lie shallow in hurried graves,
dressed by their elders in the garb of war.
Accoutrements of leather and steel
sink with their bones
as they settle to their endless sleep
nourishing the earth with their unlived years.

You look in sadness and anger
at the bloodied hair and torn uniforms
revealing cold, stilled youth.
See through my clear eyes to an innocent time
and let us be away from here.
Quickly now,
away from the approval talk old of men
with rights of death over the young.
We hurry away,
yet still we hear the bugle calls
which prise young men from reason.

Sink to the ground,
press your stomach to your knees.
Stifle the desperation in the wounded heart
and that unsated drop,
that last uncried tear
held in the tightest eye,
leave that for God to know,
for Man never will.

Peter Tomlinson spent his youth on Merseyside in the liberating 'sixties. His earliest poems were written during his army service overseas. He describes himself as loitering in the byways of thought probing the spaces between ideas. His poetry is readily accessible to the reader: dealing with pathos, beauty, irony and memory. He also writes short stories, epigrams and novels.